QUICK & EASY KETO COOKBOOK

Effortless Low-Carb Recipes for
Busy Lifestyles, Simplifying Your
Journey to Health and Flavorful
Eating

Joseph J. Easley

1

Copyright©Joseph J. Easley

TABLE OF CONTENT

INTRODUCTION

The Ketogenic Diet: An Extensive Introduction to Keto

In order to encourage your body to burn fat for energy, the ketogenic diet calls for ingesting very little in the way of carbs and substituting them with fat. Losing weight and reducing your risk of certain illnesses are two health advantages.

The ketogenic diet, often known as the low-carb, high-fat diet, has many health advantages.

Actually, a number of studies indicate that following this kind of diet might help you become healthier and lose weight.

Ketogenic diets may potentially be beneficial in the fight against Alzheimer's disease, diabetes, cancer, and epilepsy.

What are the fundamental keto guidelines?

Basics of keto

The Atkins and low-carb diets are comparable to the ketogenic diet in that they are both very low in carbohydrates and rich in fat.

It entails cutting down on carbohydrates significantly and substituting fat for them. When you cut down on carbohydrates, your body enters a metabolic condition known as ketosis.

Your body becomes very adept at burning fat for energy when this occurs. Additionally, it causes the liver to produce ketones from fat, which the brain may use as fuel.

Blood sugar and insulin levels may drop significantly while following a ketogenic diet. This has several health advantages in addition to the elevated ketones.

The ketogenic diet is a high-fat, low-carb diet. It also causes a change in the body's metabolism from burning carbohydrates to burning fat and ketones, lowering blood sugar and insulin levels.

What foods fit within a ketogenic diet?

The ketogenic diet comes in several forms, and the one you follow will determine what you consume. Among them are:

The standard ketogenic diet (SKD) consists of a high-fat, moderate-protein, and very low-carb diet. Usually, it has 10% carbohydrates, 20% protein, and 70% fat.

The cyclical ketogenic diet (CKD) alternates two days of high-carbohydrate eating with five days of ketogenic eating.

Targeted ketogenic diet (TKD): You may increase your intake of carbohydrates in relation to your exercise.

Similar to a conventional ketogenic diet, but with additional protein, is the high-protein ketogenic diet. Typically, the ratio is 35% protein, 5% carbohydrates, and 60% fat.

Only the conventional and high-protein ketogenic diets, however, have undergone substantial research. Bodybuilders and athletes are the main users of cyclical or targeted ketogenic diets, which are more sophisticated approaches.

Although many of the same concepts also apply to the other variations, the majority of the material on this page is relevant to the standard ketogenic diet (SKD).

The keto diet comes in several forms. The most extensively studied and highly advised variant is the standard (SKD) version.

What is the state of ketosis?

When your body is in a ketogenic state, it burns fat rather than carbohydrates as fuel.

It happens when you drastically cut down on the amount of carbs you eat, which limits your body's production of glucose, or sugar, which is the primary energy source for cells.

The best approach to getting into ketosis is to follow a ketogenic diet. This usually entails consuming no more than 20 to 50 grams of carbohydrates per day and consuming enough fat from foods like meat, fish, eggs, nuts, and healthy oils.

It's crucial to control your intake of protein. This is due to the fact that consuming large quantities of protein might cause it to be turned into glucose, which could delay your body's entry into ketosis.

You may be able to reach ketosis more quickly by engaging in intermittent fasting. Although there are various variations on intermittent fasting, the most popular approach is to eat for no more than eight hours a day and fast for the remaining sixteen.

There are tests for blood, urine, and breath that may measure the quantity of ketones your body produces to help identify whether you've entered ketosis.

Other signs that you may be in ketosis include reduced appetite or hunger, frequent urination, dry mouth, and increased thirst.

When your body is in a ketogenic state, it burns fat rather than carbohydrates as fuel. You may achieve ketosis more quickly by altering your diet and engaging in intermittent fasting. Determining if you've entered ketosis may also be aided by a few tests and symptoms.

Can I lose weight with the ketogenic diet?

A ketogenic diet may help you reduce your risk of illness and lose weight.

Actually, studies suggest that the ketogenic diet could be just as successful in helping people lose weight as a low-fat diet.

Furthermore, you may lose weight on this diet without measuring your food consumption or calorie intake, since it is quite satisfying.

A very low-carb, ketogenic diet was shown to be marginally more successful for long-term weight reduction than a low-fat diet in an analysis of 13 studies. The ketogenic diet group shed an average of 2 pounds (0.9 kg) more weight than the low-fat diet group.

Moreover, it resulted in reductions in lipid and diastolic blood pressure.

In another study, participants on an 8-week ketogenic diet lost almost five times as much total body fat as those on a low-fat diet, including 34 older individuals.

Additionally, important factors might be elevated ketones, decreased blood sugar, and enhanced insulin sensitivity.

You may lose a little bit more weight with a ketogenic diet than with a low-fat diet. Less hunger is often the cause of this.

Does the ketogenic diet benefit those who have prediabetes or diabetes?

Changes in metabolism, elevated blood sugar, and compromised insulin activity are the hallmarks of diabetes.

You may reduce extra fat, which is strongly associated with type 2 diabetes, prediabetes, and metabolic syndrome, by following a ketogenic diet.

An earlier study discovered a staggering 75% increase in insulin sensitivity while following a ketogenic diet.

Additionally, a 90-day ketogenic diet dramatically lowered hemoglobin A1C levels, a gauge of long-term blood sugar control, in a small trial of women with type 2 diabetes.

Over the course of two years, participants in a different trial, including 349 individuals with type 2 diabetes who followed a ketogenic diet, dropped an average of 26.2 pounds (11.9 kg). Taking into account the connection between type 2 diabetes and weight, this is a significant advantage.

Additionally, throughout the course of the trial, individuals' blood sugar control improved and their usage of certain blood sugar drugs dropped.

See this article on the advantages of low-carb diets for diabetics for further details.

For those with type 2 diabetes or prediabetes, the ketogenic diet may increase insulin sensitivity and promote fat reduction, which will have a major positive impact on their health.

What additional advantages does the ketogenic diet offer?

In actuality, the ketogenic diet was developed as a technique to treat neurological conditions like epilepsy.

Research has now shown that the diet may be beneficial for a broad range of conditions, including:

heart conditions. Risk factors such as blood pressure, blood sugar, body fat, and HDL (good) cholesterol levels may all be improved with the ketogenic diet.

Cancer. Dietary interventions for cancer are now being investigated since they may help delay the development of tumors.

seizures. Studies have shown that children with epilepsy may significantly reduce their seizure frequency when following a ketogenic diet.

Parkinson's illness. One study revealed that the diet helped reduce Parkinson's disease symptoms, while additional research is required.

Numerous health advantages, particularly in cases of metabolic, neurological, or insulin-related illnesses, may be obtained from a ketogenic diet.

On a ketogenic diet, what foods should I avoid?

Eat less of any meal that is heavy in carbohydrates.

The following foods must be cut down on or avoided while following a ketogenic diet:

sugar-filled foods: candies, ice cream, cake, smoothies, fruit juice, and soda.

Grains or starches: cereal, pasta, rice, and other wheat-based goods.

fruit: every fruit, with the exception of little amounts of berries like strawberries.

legumes, such as kidney beans, chickpeas, lentils, peas, etc.

Sweet potatoes, parsnips, carrots, and potatoes are examples of root vegetables and tubers.

Low-fat condiments, salad dressings, and mayonnaise are examples of diet or low-fat goods.

a few sauces or condiments: ketchup, honey mustard, teriyaki sauce, barbecue sauce, etc.

harmful fats: mayonnaise, processed vegetable oils, etc.

alcohol: mixed drinks, wine, beer, and liquor

diet foods without added sugar, such as syrups, puddings, sweets, sweeteners, and desserts.

Steer clear of foods high in carbohydrates, such as cereals, sweets, beans, rice, potatoes, candies, juice, and even most fruits.

With our Nutrition Edition, you can master healthy eating.

Sign up for our nutrition newsletter to get three times a week of scrumptious recipes, research updates, and candid answers to your dietary questions. Rekindle your love of cuisine that lifts your spirits.

CHAPTER ONE

Chapter 1. The Keto Diet: What Is It?

The ketogenic diet plan, often known as the low-carb, high-fat diet, has gained popularity as a successful way to reduce body weight and enhance overall health and wellbeing. The main tenet of the keto diet plan is to drastically cut your intake of carbohydrates and replace it with a small amount of protein and healthy, balanced fats.

The main goal of the keto diet plan is to switch your body's primary fuel source from carbs to fats. Your body enters a condition known as ketosis as a result. Your liver produces ketones from fat while you're in ketosis, and they become your body's and your mind's main source of energy.

Numerous benefits have been linked to this metabolic state, including improved blood sugar regulation, increased energy, increased mental clarity, and fat burning. Furthermore, the ketogenic diet plan has shown encouraging results in the treatment of diseases including epilepsy, type 2 diabetes, and polycystic ovarian syndrome (PCOS).

Weight Loss: A lot of individuals use the ketogenic diet to shed additional pounds. Your body becomes more efficient at using stored fat for energy when you consume fewer carbohydrates and more fat. This results in weight control.

Mental Quality: When compared to sugar, ketones are a much more steady and dependable source of energy for your brain. This may lead to less mental fog and increased psychological focus and quality.

Increased Power Levels: An increase in energy levels is a typical advantage that keto dieters mention. Through removing the energy collisions brought on by fluctuations in blood sugar, your body maintains a steady source of fuel.

Blood Sugar Level Control: It has been shown that the ketogenic diet plan effectively controls blood sugar levels, which makes it a compelling substitute for individuals who have type 2 diabetes mellitus or want to avoid blood glucose spikes.

Additional Health Benefits: Studies indicate that the ketogenic diet plan may be beneficial for diseases including Alzheimer's disease, acne, polycystic ovarian syndrome (PCOS), and certain types of cancer. To fully understand these potential benefits, however, further study is necessary. Although the keto diet may seem new, it has been around for a long time. It originally came to light in the 1920s. At first, physicians suggested it to treat diseases like diabetes and epilepsy. However, the keto diet is being used by some individuals to reduce weight.

Carbs, such as breads, pastas, and potatoes, account for more than half of the daily diet of many Americans. The glucose (sugars) in carbohydrates are broken down by your body to provide energy.

The aim of the ketogenic diet is to replace the calories from glucose with fat. The main focus of a normal ketogenic diet is on high-fat meals. They will account for between 60% and 80% of your daily energy intake. 15%–20% are made up of proteins. The maximum amount of carbs allowed is 50 grams. It is thus a very restricted diet.

According to studies, those who follow the low-carb ketogenic diet have a higher chance of losing weight than people who follow a more balanced diet during the first three to six months of the diet. However, since the keto diet necessitates significant dietary adjustments, it's essential to see a nutritionist or doctor before beginning.

CHAPTER TWO

Chapter 2.How is the diet effective?

You're not getting enough carbohydrates while following the ketogenic diet to meet your body's energy requirements. Your body then uses the fat reserves in your body to power your energy.

Your body creates compounds called ketones in your liver when it burns fat for energy. There is a metabolic shift in your body known as "ketosis."

Your body will enter ketosis in around 4 days if you adhere to the ketogenic diet exactly. It's possible that you may lose a few pounds over the first week.

Which keto diet types are there?

Remember, there are several kinds of keto diets if you want to start one. All of them center on modest adjustments to the ratios of fat, protein, and carbohydrates in your regular diet.

Among the keto diet varieties are:

The ketogenic standard diet (SKD). This diet is heavy in fat, moderate in protein, and extremely low in carbs. In your regular diet, it usually consists of 70% fat, 20% protein, and 10% carbohydrates.

Ketogenic diet with cycles (CKD). This entails intervals of higher-carb "refeeds," such as two high-carb days after five ketogenic days.

ketogenic diet with a focus (TKD). You may add carbohydrates to your diet in between vigorous activities.

ketogenic diet high in protein (HPKD). You may have extra protein, but it's comparable to SKD. Typically, the ratio is 35% protein, 5% carbohydrates, and 60% fat.

The majority of studies and research have been done on conventional and high-protein diets. They're the most typical as well. The majority of users of the more recent focused and cyclical keto diets are bodybuilders or athletes.

Why would someone adopt a keto diet?

Initially, the main purpose of the ketogenic diet was to treat seizures in patients. Experts eventually extended the advantages to a number of other medical ailments, such as:

enhancement of memory and cognition

Diabetes type 2

tumors like glioblastoma

Mental illnesses

Alzheimer's illness

Autism

Being overweight

For certain illnesses, the keto diet has shown great promise, particularly for type 2 diabetes. In one study, 349 people with type 2 diabetes were followed for a year, and the outcomes were compared before and after the ketogenic diet. In almost 60% of cases, it restored the diabetic state. Many of the research participants found that the keto diet reduced their need for insulin prescription medications.

It is advisable to see your doctor before beginning the ketogenic diet if you have a medical issue.

How can a keto diet be started?

You may need to throw away a few items from your cupboard and add some high-fat foods to your regular meals when you first start the keto diet.

Find out what will work best for you by speaking with a nutritionist or your doctor. This is particularly crucial if you follow any other dietary restrictions, including being a vegetarian, vegan, or suffering from certain food allergies. Professionals may assist you in identifying substitutions or alternatives and creating a food plan that best meets your requirements.

CHAPTER THREE

Chapter 3.Here are some questions you should think about asking your doctor before you start making meal changes:

Will there be health issues that the keto diet will help manage?

Must you reduce your weight?

Which adverse effects are there?

Is it okay to take vitamins or supplements while on a diet?

How long is the ketogenic diet recommended to last?

Do you need to work out? How much, if at all?

What foods are allowed on a keto diet?

Among the ketogenic foods are:

Nuts

Seeds

dairy items with added fat

Greek yogurt

veggies that are fibrous and non-starchy.

fatty substances

Meat

Fish

Eggs

cottage cheese

Coconut

For your daily 20 to 50 grams of
carbohydrates, go for non-starchy
vegetables such as:

broccoli

Lettuce

Chilis

fungi

greens with leaves

Asparagus

Verdant beans

Foods that are heavy in carbohydrates and starchy (such as:

Bread

baked products

sugary candies

Pasta

Rice

cereals for breakfast

starchy vegetables such as beans, peas, maize, potatoes, and sweet potatoes

Sugar-rich fruits

Wine

Unless it's low-carb, beer

You may consume unsweetened tea or coffee while following the ketogenic diet. Reduce the amount of alcohol you consume. If you're an alcohol drinker, go for low-carb options like vodka or tequila and combine them with soda water.

What Types of Snacks Are Allowed on a Keto Diet?

Low-carb snacks that are keto-friendly include a decent ratio of healthy fats and modest protein. You may buy store-bought versions or prepare ones yourself.

This covers munchies like:

Brazil nuts

Cashews

Almonds

Almonds

Yogurt made with coconuts

Avocado

Cheese

Tuna canned

Jerky meat

Olives

Risers of pork

Seaweed appetizers

Hard-boiled eggs

Jicama is a root vegetable low in carbs.

These snacks may assist you in controlling your appetite in between meals and sustaining long-term ketosis.

Does a keto diet come with risks?

The rigorous keto diet isn't a smart option for everyone, despite evidence showing that it helps some individuals lose weight or manage medical issues. If you follow the diet improperly or without enough supervision, it might be hazardous.

Everybody responds to the keto diet in a different way. Some individuals may discover that it takes longer for their body to acclimate to the abrupt changes in food, while others may find it easier to adjust.

It's critical to have routine cholesterol testing performed. For some individuals, the ketogenic diet may lower cholesterol, while for others, it may raise cholesterol.

For some individuals, the low-carb component of the diet may have long-term effects. Cutting off carbohydrates so abruptly and severely may cause symptoms similar to the flu as your body adjusts to using fat instead of glucose for energy, a condition known as the "keto flu."

Keto flu symptoms include:

stomach discomfort or aches.

emesis

lightheadedness

yearning for sugar

stumbling

aches in the muscles

I'm grumpy

Constipation or diarrhea

Difficulties getting to sleep or staying asleep

inadequate attention and focus

fog in the brain

The symptoms of the keto flu often appear one or two days after you stop eating carbohydrates. In extreme situations, they may persist for up to a month, while they may last as little as a week. Consult your physician if the symptoms are severe or continue, and discontinue the diet.

Reduce your risk of experiencing the keto flu by beginning the diet gradually, drinking plenty of water, exercising moderately, and getting plenty of rest as your body adjusts to your new eating schedule.

Experts also caution against the fact that there are too many variations of the keto diet and that following one poorly is simple. Instead of consuming enough good fats, you can wind up eating too much saturated fat, which increases your risk of heart disease and high levels of harmful cholesterol. If you don't adhere to the diet exactly, you could not achieve ketosis either.

Your gut health may be impacted by the ketogenic diet. This is due to the fact that the diet primarily calls for eliminating foods high in fiber and nutrients, such as fruits, whole grains, legumes, and starchy vegetables. There is inconsistent research on how keto affects gut health. Further investigation is required on this subject.

CHAPTER FOUR

Chapter 4.Knowing the Macronutrients and Food Options of the Keto Diet Regimen

It is essential to comprehend the macronutrient makeup of the foods you consume in order to follow the keto diet plan successfully. A ketogenic diet plan's typical macronutrient allocation follows this:

Fat: You should get between 70 and 75 percent of your daily energy from balanced, healthful fats. These include avocados, almonds, seeds, olive and coconut oils, and fatty meats like diaform.

Protein: You should get 20–25% of your daily calories from high-quality protein sources, which include fish, poultry, lean meats, and plant-based protein alternatives.

Carbohydrates: You should still consume 5–10% of your daily calories from carbohydrates. But it's important to choose nutrient-dense, low-carb meals like leafy greens, non-starchy veggies, and small amounts of berries.

By focusing on these macronutrient ratios, you can ensure that you are consuming the right amount of healthy fats and proteins while also keeping your carbohydrate intake low enough to induce ketosis.

Possible Hazards and Things to Think About

Although there are many benefits to the ketogenic diet plan, it's vital to be aware of any possible risks and adverse effects associated with this dietary strategy.

One common side effect, especially in the early stages of the change, is the "keto flu," a transient state that arises when your body adjusts to using ketones instead of glucose as fuel. Lightheadedness, irritability, migraines, and exhaustion are possible symptoms. However, these indications and symptoms often go away within a few days or many weeks.

Another thing to think about is that not everyone should follow a ketogenic diet. Individuals who suffer from certain medical issues, such as liver disease, pancreatitis, or a history of eating disorders, should avoid the ketogenic diet or approach it cautiously. Furthermore, women who are nursing or expecting should see their doctor before making any dietary changes.

Moreover, the restricted nature of the keto diet plan may make it difficult to follow for an extended period of time. It may be challenging to adhere to in certain social situations or while dining in restaurants, as it requires careful meal preparation and may restrict your food options.

The ketogenic diet plan has really drawn a lot of attention lately due to its potential advantages for improving overall wellbeing, psychological quality, and weight reduction. Your body enters a state of ketosis, where it runs entirely on fat instead of carbohydrates, by drastically cutting down on carbs.

It is important to remember that not everyone can follow the keto diet plan, and there may be hazards and negative consequences to take into account. It is advisable to speak with a healthcare professional before making any major dietary changes.

Whether the keto diet is the right option for you ultimately depends on a variety of variables, such as your lifestyle, health goals, and personal preferences. To maintain a healthy and well-balanced lifestyle over the long term, it is essential to learn about different dietary approaches and figure out what works best for your body.

What's That?

A low-carb diet (similar to the Atkins diet) is referred to as "ketogenic." The goal is for you to consume fewer carbs and more fat and protein in your diet. The easiest carbohydrates to digest, such as sugar, soda, pastries, and white bread, are the ones you reduce the most.

How It Operates

Less than 50 grams of carbohydrates per day causes your body to soon run out of blood sugar, which is fuel. Usually, this takes three or four days. After that, you'll begin to burn fat and protein for energy, which may help you lose weight. We refer to this as ketosis. It's crucial to remember that the ketogenic diet is a transient eating plan that prioritizes weight reduction above long-term health advantages.

Who makes use of it?

A ketogenic diet is most often used to help people lose weight, but it may also be used to treat specific medical disorders, including epilepsy. More study is needed in the fields of heart illness, certain brain ailments, and even acne, since these conditions may benefit from its use. If you have type 1 diabetes in particular, check with your doctor to see whether you may safely attempt a ketogenic diet.

Loss of weight

Compared to some other diets, a ketogenic diet could help you lose more weight in the first three to six months. This might be the case since burning fat requires more calories than burning carbohydrates to produce energy. Though it hasn't been proven, it's also plausible that eating a high-fat, high-protein diet makes you feel more satisfied, which leads to less eating.

Cancer

The hormone insulin enables your body to either store or utilize sugar as fuel. You don't need to store this fuel since a ketogenic diet causes you to burn through it rapidly. This indicates that your body produces less insulin than it needs to. These reduced levels could even inhibit the development of cancer cells, helping to protect you against some types of cancer.

However, further study is required in this area.

Heart Conditions

It may seem unusual that eating more fat might increase good cholesterol and decrease bad cholesterol, yet that is exactly what ketogenic diets have been shown to do. It could be because these diets lead your body to produce less insulin, which can prevent your body from producing more cholesterol. This implies that you have a lower risk of developing heart failure, hardened arteries, high blood pressure, and other cardiac disorders. However, it's unknown how long these benefits endure.

Unknown

Reducing your intake of carbohydrates may be beneficial since they have been connected to this skin issue. Furthermore, a ketogenic diet may prevent acne by causing a reduction in insulin. (Insulin may trigger the production of other hormones that exacerbate breakouts.) Nevertheless, more investigation is required to pinpoint the precise impact, if any, of the diet on acne.

Diabetes

Compared to other diets, low-carb diets seem to help maintain more stability and lower blood sugar levels. However, your body produces substances known as ketones when it consumes fat for energy. Being unwell from having too many ketones in your blood may happen to people with diabetes, especially type 1. Therefore, it's crucial that you discuss any dietary modifications with your doctor.

seizures

Since the 1920s, ketogenic diets have been employed to help reduce seizures brought on by this illness. Once again, however, it's critical to collaborate with your physician to determine what's best for you or your child.

These impact not just your spine and brain but also the nerves that connect them. A ketogenic diet may be beneficial for conditions such as epilepsy, Parkinson's disease, Alzheimer's disease, and sleep disturbances. It's possible that the ketones your body produces while it burns fat for energy might shield your brain cells from harm, but scientists aren't sure why.

Ovary Polycystic Syndrome

This is the process by which a woman's ovaries enlarge beyond normal, and tiny sacs packed with fluid surround the eggs. It may result from high insulin levels. Along with other lifestyle modifications like exercise and weight reduction, ketogenic diets, which reduce the amount of insulin you create and require, may help treat it.

Work out

When training, endurance athletes like cyclists and runners may benefit from a ketogenic diet. It eventually improves your muscle-to-fat ratio and increases the quantity of oxygen your body can use during intense exercise. For peak performance, however, it may not be as effective as other diets, even if it can be helpful in training.

Adverse Reactions

The more frequent ones, such as indigestion, mildly low blood sugar, or constipation, are typically not significant. Low-carb diets are far less likely to cause kidney stones, acidosis, or elevated acidity in the body. The "keto flu," which may include headache, weakness, and irritability as well as weariness and foul breath, is another possible adverse effect.

Eat Cautiously

Your kidneys may suffer as a result of your body burning up its fat reserves. It might also be difficult to begin a ketogenic diet and then return to a regular diet if you are obese due to comorbid conditions such as diabetes, high blood pressure, or heart disease. If you suffer from any of these ailments, alter your diet gradually and only under your doctor's supervision.

Which foods fit within the ketogenic diet?

The bulk of your meals have to revolve around these foods:

Meat includes turkey, ham, sausage, bacon, chicken, and red meat.

fatty fish, such as mackerel, salmon, trout, and tuna.

pastured or whole eggs with omega-3

Cream and butter: rich, grass-fed cream and butter

cheese: natural cheeses such as mozzarella, cheddar, goat, cream, or blue.

Nuts and seeds: chia seeds, flaxseeds, pumpkin seeds, walnuts, almonds, etc.

Extra virgin olive oil and avocado oil are healthful oils.

avocados: either raw or freshly prepared guacamole

vegetables low in carbohydrates: peppers, tomatoes, onions, and greens.

Condiments include spices, herbs, salt, and pepper.

It is advisable to consume mostly entire meals made of one component. This is a list of forty-four nutritious low-carb foods.

Make meat, fish, eggs, butter, nuts, healthy oils, avocados, and an abundance of low-carb vegetables the main components of your diet.

A weeklong keto eating plan example

Here is an example weekly meal plan for the ketogenic diet to get you started:

Monday

Vegetable and egg muffins with tomatoes for breakfast

Lunch is a side salad with feta cheese, olives, and chicken salad dressed with olive oil.

Dinner is butter-sautéed asparagus and fish.

Tuesday

Egg, tomato, basil, and spinach omelet for breakfast

Lunch consists of a stevia milkshake, almond milk, peanut butter, spinach, chocolate powder, and sliced strawberries on the side. See more keto smoothie recipes here.

Dinner is salsa-topped cheese-shell tacos.

Wednesday

Breakfast is chia pudding with nut milk, coconut, and blackberries on top.

avocado shrimp salad for lunch

Dinner is salad, broccoli, and pork chops with Parmesan cheese.

Thursday

Avocado, salsa, peppers, onions, and spices in an omelet for breakfast

For lunch, have some almonds and celery sticks with salsa and guacamole.

Dinner consists of grilled zucchini on the side and chicken packed with cream cheese and pesto.

Friday

Breakfast consists of whole milk Greek yogurt without added sugar, fruit, peanut butter, or chocolate powder.

Lunch is tacos made with ground beef, lettuce, and sliced bell peppers.

Supper is mixed vegetables and stuffed cauliflower.

On Saturday

Cream cheese pancakes with blueberries
and grilled mushrooms on the side for
breakfast

Lunch is a salad of zucchini and beets.

Dinner includes greens, toasted pine nuts,
and white fish fried in olive oil.

Sunday

Breakfast consists of fried eggs and
mushrooms.

Lunch would be veggies and low-carb
sesame chicken.

Dinner is bolognese spaghetti squash.

Over time, aim to alternate your meat and vegetables since each variety offers unique nutrients and health advantages.

See this keto shopping list and these 101 healthy low-carb recipes for a ton of meal ideas.

On a ketogenic diet, you may enjoy a broad range of delectable and nourishing meals. Not everything is meat and fat. An essential component of every diet is vegetables.

wholesome keto snacks

In case you find yourself starving in between meals, consider these nutritious, keto-approved snacks:

Fish or meat with high fat content

cheese

a little handful of seeds or nuts

keto sushi nibbles

olives

one or two eggs, deviled or hard-boiled

Keto-friendly snack bars

90% cocoa solid

nuts and chocolate powder combined with
full-fat Greek yogurt

Guacamole with bell peppers

simple cottage cheese with strawberries

Carrots with guacamole and salsa

Jerky made with beef

reduced serving sizes of leftover food

fatty bombs

Meat chunks, cheese, olives, boiled eggs, almonds, raw vegetables, and dark chocolate are all excellent keto snack options.

Keto advice and techniques

While beginning a ketogenic diet might be difficult, there are a few strategies you can use to make it simpler.

To figure out how your favorite foods may fit into your diet, start by becoming acquainted with food labels and looking up the grams of fat, carbohydrates, and fiber.

It might be advantageous to plan your meals ahead of time to save additional time throughout the week.

You may create your own personalized menu by using the many websites, food blogs, apps, and cookbooks that provide keto-friendly recipes and meal ideas.

As an alternative, several meal delivery services also include keto-friendly selections, making it simple and easy to eat keto at home.

When you're pressed for time, consider frozen keto meals that are healthy.

You may also want to think about packing your own meals for social events or trips to see loved ones. This might help you resist temptations and follow your meal plan.

Sticking to the ketogenic diet may be made much simpler by reading food labels, preparing meals, and carrying your own food while visiting family and friends.

Advice for ketogenic diet diners

You can make a lot of restaurant dishes keto-friendly.

Most eateries include some kind of meal that includes meat or seafood. Order this and add more veggies in lieu of any foods high in carbohydrates.

Egg-based dishes, such as omelets or eggs with bacon, are also excellent choices.

Another favorite are burgers without buns. Vegetables might be substituted for the fries. Add more eggs, bacon, cheese, avocado, or cheese.

Any kind of meat may be enjoyed in Mexican restaurants with additional cheese, guacamole, salsa, and sour cream.

Request berries with cream or a mixed cheese platter for dessert.

Choose a food that is either meat-, fish-, or egg-based while dining out. Order more vegetables rather than breads or pastas, and for dessert, have cheese.

Side effects: ways to reduce them

As most healthy individuals may safely follow a ketogenic diet, there may be some early adverse effects as your body adjusts.

These consequences, also known as the "keto flu," have been seen in some cases.

Some on the eating regimen have reported that it normally ends after a few days.

The symptoms of the keto flu that have been reported include vomiting, constipation, and diarrhea.

Other, less typical symptoms consist of:

low vitality and cognitive abilities

heightened appetite

problems sleeping

nausea

stomach ache

reduced effectiveness of exercise

You may attempt a standard low-carb diet for the first few weeks to lessen this. If you do this, your body could learn to burn more fat before you cut off all carbohydrates.

Adding more salt to your food or taking mineral supplements may assist, since a ketogenic diet may also alter your body's water and mineral balance. Discuss your dietary requirements with your physician.

It is crucial to eat until you are satisfied and refrain from severely limiting your calorie intake, especially in the beginning. A ketogenic diet often results in weight reduction without purposeful calorie limitation.

You can minimize a lot of the negative impacts of beginning a ketogenic diet.

Supplementing with minerals and easing into the diet might be beneficial.

CHAPTER FIVE

Chapter 5.Does following a ketogenic diet have any risks?

Although the ketogenic diet has many advantages, following it for an extended period of time may have certain drawbacks.

includes the following dangers:

low blood protein levels

surplus fat in the liver

kidney stones

deficits in micronutrients

Sodium-glucose cotransporter 2 (SGLT2) inhibitors are a kind of medicine used to treat type 2 diabetes that may raise the risk of diabetic ketoacidosis, a hazardous disease that causes blood acidity to rise. The ketogenic diet should be avoided by anyone on this medicine.

To ascertain the long-term safety of the ketogenic diet, further study is being conducted. To help you make decisions, let your doctor know about your diet.

If you want to follow the ketogenic diet for an extended period of time, you should talk to your doctor about the negative effects of the diet.

Are there ketogenic diet supplements available?

Supplements are not necessary; however, some may be helpful.

MCT grease. MCT oil raises ketone levels and gives energy when added to beverages or yogurt. Get MCT oil online.

minerals. Changes in the water and mineral balance might make added salt and other minerals crucial when first starting out.

Coffee. There are advantages to caffeine for performance, energy, and fat reduction.

ketones that are not exogenous. The body's ketone levels may be elevated by taking this supplement.

Get creatine. There are many advantages to creatine for performance and wellness. If you combine exercise with a ketogenic diet, this may be beneficial.

Whey. To boost your daily protein consumption, add half a scoop of whey protein to smoothies or yogurt.

When following a ketogenic diet, several supplements may be helpful. These consist of micronutrients, MCT oil, and exogenous ketones.

Frequently requested inquiries

These are some of the frequently asked questions about the ketogenic diet and their responses.

Can I ever have carbohydrates again?

Indeed. But it's crucial to start out with much lower carbohydrate consumption. You may have carbohydrates on special occasions after the first two to three months; just make sure you quickly go back on the diet.

Will my muscular mass diminish?

Any diet carries some danger of muscle loss. However, if you workout, eating a lot of protein and having high ketone levels may help reduce muscle loss.

Can a ketogenic diet help me gain muscle?

Yes, however, it may not function as effectively as a diet low in carbohydrates.

What is my daily protein intake?

Moderate protein consumption is recommended since excessive protein may diminish ketones and raise insulin levels. The top limit is probably around 35 percent of the total calories consumed.

What if I feel weak, exhausted, or weary all the time?

It's possible that you're not fully in ketosis or making optimal use of fats and ketones. Reduce your carbohydrate consumption and go over the previously mentioned recommendations to combat this. Supplements such as ketones or MCT oil may also be beneficial.

There's a fragrance on my breath. How am I able to help?

This is a typical adverse reaction. Try sucking on sugar-free gum or sipping naturally flavored water.

I'd heard ketosis was quite risky. Is this accurate?

Ketosis and ketoacidosis are sometimes confused by people. While ketosis on a ketogenic diet is generally safe for healthy individuals, ketoacidosis is harmful. Consult your physician prior to beginning any new diet.

I get diarrhea and stomach problems. How am I able to help?

This typical side effect normally goes away in three to four weeks. Try consuming additional high-fiber vegetables if it continues.

What distinguishes a ketogenic diet from a non-ketogenic diet?

The keto diet and the ketogenic diet are interchangeable words that are often used in casual speech.

With keto, how much weight can I lose in a week?

During the first week of the ketogenic diet, water weight is usually lost. Anecdotally, individuals claim to have lost anything from 1 lb (0.5 kg) to 10 lb or more (5 kg).

Learn more about losing weight on a ketogenic diet after a week.

Is a ketogenic diet beneficial to you?

A ketogenic diet could be very beneficial for those who:

are oversized

possess diabetes

want to enhance their metabolic well-being.

For top athletes or those looking to gain significant muscle or weight, it may not be as appropriate.

Additionally, it could not fit the tastes and lives of some individuals. To find out whether a ketogenic diet is best for you, discuss your objectives and eating plan with your physician.

When on a ketogenic diet, you consume fewer carbohydrates and more healthy fats in their place. This may promote weight reduction and lower your risk of developing certain health problems by helping your body use fat as fuel.

Nevertheless, before committing to the diet for a long period of time, speak with your doctor since it could have some adverse consequences. To fully comprehend its long-term effects on the body, further study is required.

Items I Should Have Known Before Beginning the Keto Diet

I was about to be married a few years ago, and I wanted to shed some pounds. Even though I was exercising and eating well, I wasn't getting the noticeable results I was hoping for. I made the decision to attempt a different diet for a few weeks: the ketogenic, or "keto" diet. I did drop more than a pound per week when I followed it for three weeks and lost 3.5 pounds. However, there are undoubtedly certain things I should have known before giving up carbohydrates.

Is there really a healthy keto diet plan?

At first, you'll probably feel horrible.

After going keto for a few days, I experienced the "keto flu," which is caused by a sharp drop in electrolyte levels in the body. Getting a decent balance of salt, magnesium, and potassium on the ketogenic diet may be challenging since these nutrients are mostly found in meals high in carbohydrates, such as beans, fruit, and potatoes. Headaches, nausea, fatigue, and mental fog are some of the symptoms of the keto flu. It wasn't enjoyable at all; for me, it felt like the start of a cold, when your body feels physically heavy and worn out.

CHAPTER SIX

Chapter .6 You must make plans.

The keto diet has the benefit of not requiring you to manage calories, points, or macros—all you have to do is keep an eye on your net carbohydrates, which are your total carbohydrates less fiber. However, if you want to stay away from the unpleasant symptoms of the keto flu and maintain optimal bodily function, you should consume a lot of foods rich in potassium (such as salmon, avocado, and leafy greens) and magnesium (such as almonds, spinach, and peanut butter). Additionally, it's critical to check your fiber intake, which may be difficult to do while avoiding foods like whole grains, potatoes, and fruit.

Health professionals oppose it.

Unless you have a particular medical issue (like epilepsy) and your doctor or registered dietitian has suggested the ketogenic diet and is carefully monitoring you throughout the diet, the majority of dietitians think that it is one of the worst diets. Since poor gut health is connected to chronic illness, anxiety, inflammation, and other issues, one gastroenterologist and gut health specialist I talked with feels that keto "decimates the gut" and may be detrimental for your general health. Make sure you're getting enough fiber from plant sources, such as leafy greens, chia seeds, nuts, and berries, if you're determined to follow the ketogenic diet. The current recommendations for nutrition state that males should consume at least 38 grams per day and women should consume 28 grams.

You'll have severe cravings.

My desires were strong throughout my brief ketogenic diet. Furthermore, they never really ceased. I was craving meals that are high in carbohydrates, like warm bread, fruit, and french fries, but I was also craving items that I don't really enjoy or eat often, like Sour Patch Kids and old-fashioned cake donuts. I have no idea why this is happening, but I put it down to giving up sweets and carbohydrates completely. Restricting food might also increase your need for it. Dreaming about carbohydrates made sense since I wasn't really consuming any throughout my ketogenic diet. Even though I made an attempt to prepare low-carb versions of my favorite dishes, they were simply not the same. Cauliflower will never be bread, and zoodles will never be pasta (sorry, not sorry).

Everybody's experience is unique.

I attempted the keto diet concurrently with my spouse, and our experiences were quite different. His A1C readings improved and his blood sugar steadied; however, if you have type 1 diabetes, see your physician or nutritionist before beginning a ketogenic diet. He enjoyed eating a diet high in meat and fat, but I needed to clean my teeth many times a day to remove the taste of fat from my mouth. He felt like he had more energy and had shed almost five pounds in three weeks, whereas I felt bloated and filthy.

I also felt certain feelings connected to eating that I wasn't really ready for. At most meals, I found it difficult to consume rich and fatty foods like cheese, butter, cream cheese, and red meat since they seemed "unnatural" and "shouldn't" be a part of my weight-loss strategy. It forced me to take a step back and assess how I felt about things like red meat and butter since I had previously attempted diets that emphasized foods like veggies, lean meats, and good grains while restricting intake of these items. It was a bit unsettling that I had vilified certain things and hadn't recognized it until I was eating them on a daily basis, even though I now know that all foods have a place in a balanced diet. It turns out that, while I like them in reduced amounts, butter, cheese, and steak are favorites of mine and are now a regular part of my diet.

There could be odd side effects for you.

I couldn't get rid of the impression that fat was coating my tongue, as I already described (yuck). "Keto breath" is a transient ailment that some other keto dieters have also complained about. It might seem like an acetone-like metallic taste in your mouth or breath. It truly indicates that you are in ketosis, as it occurs when your body produces ketones as a result of burning fat. However, stomach issues are perhaps one of the most typical adverse effects (apart from the keto flu). Significant constipation, bloating, or diarrhea may be caused by drastically cutting down on your consumption of carbohydrates, not obtaining enough fiber, or consuming more fat. Make sure you consume a lot of meals high in fiber and drink a lot of water to keep things running properly.

You might put it back on.

If you go back to eating carbohydrates, the weight you lost on the ketogenic diet may come back just as rapidly. People following a low-carb or ketogenic diet lose a lot of water weight, which contributes to their rapid weight loss (each gram of carbohydrates is stored by our systems alongside around 4 g of water). Resuming carbohydrate consumption may cause those water-weight pounds to return. And since keto is so restricted, it's not practical for most individuals to follow it for life.

CHAPTER SEVEN

Chapter 7.The Complete Beginner's Guide to the Ketogenic Diet

Considering going keto? You've undoubtedly heard about some of the incredible outcomes that others have seen with the keto diet, or you may have personally witnessed them with a friend, family member, or colleague.

The low-carb keto diet is especially beneficial for those attempting to reduce weight or enhance their metabolic health. It may assist you in controlling your appetite, lowering blood sugar, and burning stored fat. There could even be some advantages to brain health from keto.

Everything you need to know about the keto diet for beginners, including what to eat and what not to, how to get started, and an example three-day keto diet plan, is covered in this article.

The Ketogenic Diet: What Is It?

The ketogenic diet consists of moderate amounts of protein, fat, and minimal carbs. Micronutrients, or the parts of food that supply calories, include protein, fat, and carbs. Most ketogenic individuals often strive for this macro breakdown:

Carbs: 5% or less of total calories

20–25% of calories are from protein.

Calorie content: 70–75% fat

This equates to around 25–50 grams of carbohydrates per day for many individuals.

Bread, pasta, potatoes, sugar-filled drinks, and even fruit are examples of foods high in carbohydrates that cause your blood sugar levels to rise.

While fat and protein may also alter your blood sugar levels, their effects are much less pronounced than those of carbohydrates.

You may achieve ketosis, a metabolic condition when your carbohydrate consumption is dramatically reduced, by following this approach. Just below, you can learn more about the advantages of ketosis.

How Do You Follow a Ketogenic Diet?

The way the keto diet works is by enabling your body to enter a condition known as ketosis.

While in ketosis, the body uses fat as its main energy source rather than the carbohydrates it typically burns for energy.

Your body may utilize body fat that has been stored or from food as fuel while it is in ketosis.

The ketogenic diet may also aid in preserving lean muscle mass and lowering hunger. This makes keto especially beneficial if losing weight is your main objective.

Various Ketogenic Diet Types

There are several varieties of ketogenic diets, and each one can be more beneficial to certain individuals than others or provide a different set of advantages. Here's a brief summary:

Standard: This is a standard keto diet, where you probably measure your food intake and follow the same daily macro pattern.

Clean: When following a ketogenic diet, you should adhere to low-carb, high-fat macronutrient patterns while avoiding overly processed meals and opting for high-quality, organic items. Fast food, prepackaged snacks, artificial sweeteners, and seed oils like soybean and maize oil are often avoided by those following a clean ketogenic diet.

Dirty keto is a keto diet that doesn't care about the quality of the foods you eat as long as you meet your macro targets. Fast food, diet drinks, artificial sweeteners, and seed oils are examples of items that may be included in a filthy keto diet.

Lazy: When you follow a ketogenic diet without monitoring your consumption, it's referred to as "lazy keto." If you don't enjoy monitoring or calculating quantities, this can work well for you. However, if weight reduction is your main aim, it might be problematic to consume too many calories or carbohydrates while on a lazy ketogenic diet.

High-Protein Keto: This variation of the ketogenic diet involves consuming at least thirty to thirty-three percent of its calories from protein (and less from fat). If you're attempting to lose weight, high-protein keto can be an excellent choice for you since protein can be quite beneficial.

Cyclical Keto: With cyclical keto, you adhere to a rigorous keto diet on some days and a higher-carb diet on others. People who have training days when they can eat more carbohydrates and ladies who wish to modify their macro consumption during their monthly cycle for hormonal balance may find this very helpful.

Targeted: Targeted keto is a variation of cyclical keto where you add pre-exercise carbohydrates before each and every workout, as opposed to providing carbohydrates just on certain days. It is simpler to maintain ketosis when these carbohydrates are burned off during exercise; however, they do offer you an extra energy and performance boost. Active individuals may benefit from targeted keto.

Additionally, there may be some overlap among these kinds. For example, you may decide to adopt a clean, lazy, cyclical keto diet, which essentially entails choosing minimally processed meals, not monitoring your macronutrient intake, and having a higher carbohydrate intake on some days.

Possible Health Advantages of a Ketogenic Diet

Blood sugar management, cognitive health, and weight reduction are the main advantages of the ketogenic diet. Significantly reducing inflammation is one of the numerous advantages of the ketogenic diet, and it is believed to have this impact in large part.

Because of this, ketogenic diets are now quite popular in the scientific community, and several recent studies have discovered evidence to support these advantages. Online, there are hundreds of testimonies of people who have experienced much better health thanks to keto.

Loss of weight

A common reason why individuals attempt keto is to reduce weight. Thousands, if not tens of thousands, of success stories of individuals who used the keto diet to achieve their weight reduction objectives can be found with a fast internet search.

Additionally, there are a few scientifically supported benefits of keto for those attempting to reduce weight:

Fat loss: Your body is more likely to burn fat in ketosis than carbohydrates, so it might be simpler to burn the fat you've accumulated.

Sparing of muscle: Keto diets have the potential to stop muscle loss during weight reduction. This keeps your metabolic rate stable, allowing you to burn the same number of calories even while your weight drops.

Diminished appetite: Many individuals claim that while on keto, their hunger is much better regulated than when eating meals rich in carbohydrates since fat and protein are more filling.

Improved blood sugar regulation: Lastly, ketogenic diets may help to balance blood sugar, which may help to manage hunger and lessen cravings for carbohydrates.

Brain Activity

Children with drug-resistant epilepsy have traditionally benefited from the use of ketogenic diets in treatment.

Ketosis seems to be quite beneficial for other elements of brain function as well, particularly for specific disorders; however, research on these aspects is currently underway.

Researchers have discovered that a ketogenic diet may be beneficial for mood disorders like depression, mental diseases like schizophrenia and bipolar disorder, and cognitive decline in addition to epilepsy and other seizure disorders.

CHAPTER EIGHT

Chapter 8.Blood sugar regulation

A lot of individuals experiment with keto to aid with blood sugar regulation. Many success stories of individuals using keto to cure type 2 diabetes or get to a stage where they don't require insulin or blood sugar-lowering drugs can be found online.

Furthermore, studies indicate that ketogenic diets may help reduce insulin resistance and blood sugar levels.

Along with other disorders linked to insulin resistance and blood sugar regulation, such as metabolic syndrome and polycystic ovarian syndrome (PCOS), keto may be helpful for type 2 diabetes.

Foods to Include in a Ketogenic Diet

You may include these meals in your keto diet plan since they are keto-friendly. Though it would be hard to list them all here, keep in mind to read the nutrition and ingredient labels for any packaged "keto" goods to determine whether they are indeed keto-friendly.

Meats and proteins include pork, eggs, soybeans, soy proteins, fish, poultry, turkey, beef, chicken, and turkey.

Fruits: coconut, lime juice, coconut juice, raspberries, and strawberries

Vegetables: bell peppers, chili peppers, radishes, cucumbers, okra, mushrooms, green beans, spinach, kale, bok choy, carrots, celery, broccoli, zucchini, cauliflower, collard greens, mustard greens, lettuce, cabbage, arugula, yellow squash, garlic, and tomato (in small portions).

dairy items, such as cheese, sour cream, and cream cheese.

Alternatives to dairy include unsweetened plant milks (almond, soy, and coconut).

Nuts and seeds: macadamia nuts, hazelnuts, pecans, almonds, walnuts, sesame seeds, chia seeds, and flax seeds

Butter, culinary oils, coconut oil, animal fats, and other fats and oils

Other: herbs, spices, sugar-free dark chocolate, vinegar (apart from balsamic), broths, mayonnaise, mustard, and spicy sauce

Meats and proteins: imitation crab meat, all beans and legumes (except peanuts and soybeans), breaded or fried meats

Fruits: all fruits, except those that are listed as keto-friendly.

Vegetables: peas, winter squash, maize, potatoes, and sweet potatoes.

Grains include tortillas, flatbreads, biscuits, rolls, crackers, oats, grits, bread, rice, pasta, flour, cornmeal, and quinoa.

Nuts and seeds: pistachios, cashews

Foods high in sugar include fruit juices, sugar-filled sodas, sweetened drinks, candies, cookies, cakes, snack cakes, ice cream, syrups, jellies, and honey.

dairy foods like yogurt and milk

Other: ketchup, balsamic vinegar, and sweetened coffee creamers

Never forget to read nutrition labels. Many foods have higher carbohydrate contents than you would think.

Which supplements are allowed during a keto diet?

While on keto, you don't necessarily need vitamins, although some could make you feel better. These are the suggestions we have:

Electrolytes

Minerals called electrolytes aid in controlling how well your muscles work.

When you initially start keto, you could feel tired, headachy, and have muscular cramps while your body adjusts to the new concentrations of electrolytes.

Electrolyte supplements may be quite beneficial in preventing these undesirable side effects.

Try Perfect Keto Daily Electrolytes for a nice and simple electrolyte supplement.

MCT Lubricant

The special kind of oil known as medium-chain triglyceride (MCT) oil has qualities that make it especially beneficial for ketogenic diets.

Lost your carbohydrates while on keto?

Get our best keto recipes if you like carbs.

MCT oil may help you enter a deeper state of ketosis, according to some studies, and it may also increase the amount of fat your body burns when you exercise.

Perfect Keto MCT Oil Powder is easy to use with protein shakes or your daily cup of coffee.

Powdered Protein

Having trouble getting enough protein?

An inexpensive and handy approach to increasing your protein consumption might be using protein powder.

A protein smoothie is a terrific way to get your protein fix after working out, as well as a satisfying breakfast or snack to go.

Most protein powders are keto-friendly, but you should always double-check the label, just to be sure. Perfect Keto Whey Protein, on the other hand, is specifically made for keto and has MCT oil added.

CHAPTER NINE

Chapter 9. An Example of a Keto Diet Plan

For your first few days on the keto diet, you may get some mealtime inspiration from this example three-day meal plan.

First Day

Two bacon slices and two eggs cooked in bacon grease for breakfast

Lunch is roasted broccoli and a cheese-topped bunless burger.

Supper is grilled ribeye steak with avocado-oil-sautéed asparagus and mushrooms.

Walnuts, strawberries, and unsweetened whipped cream for a snack

Day Two

Breakfast consists of a protein smoothie made with ice, half an avocado, raspberries, unsweetened almond milk, and protein powder that is suitable for keto.

Lunch is a keto taco bowl made of cauliflower rice, taco sauce, cheese, sour cream, cilantro, and lime juice, along with seasoned ground beef.

Dinner is "spaghetti" cooked with zucchini noodles, handmade meatballs, and spaghetti sauce without added sugar (no breadcrumbs).

Almonds, cheese, and hard-boiled eggs for a snack

Day Three

Omelet with spinach, mushrooms, and mozzarella cheese for breakfast

Lunch is a low-carb tortilla wrap with turkey, bacon, and avocado and a dressing created without additional sugar for the coleslaw.

Dinner is a salad made with greens, tomatoes, red onions, and ranch dressing with grilled salmon filet.

Snack: tiny carrots with sour cream dip and beef jerky without added sugar

Remember to go through our recipes for more ideas.

How to Begin Following a Ketogenic Diet

Here's how to begin a ketogenic diet.

Read up: It's crucial that you comprehend the basics thoroughly before beginning the keto diet. Any of the other materials on the Perfect Keto site, including this post, are excellent places to start. Make sure you understand how to read nutrition and ingredient labels and which items are and are not keto-friendly.

Next, you should determine your macros and create targets. What goals do you have for using keto? The better, the more precise. For instance, you may want to lose weight or stop using part of your diabetic medication. Make sure to determine your individual keto macros and whether you want to track net or total carbohydrates.

Stock your cupboard, refrigerator, and freezer with keto-friendly items to prepare for the keto diet. Eliminating high-carb items is also a smart idea if you can, since it will keep them from luring you in every time you go into the kitchen.

Prior to beginning, arrange your meals for the next week. When and what will you eat? If you decide to go out to dine, accept an invitation to a party, or find yourself working beyond your usual hours, how will you manage to stay on the ketogenic diet? Success depends on preparing for these situations in advance. To stay on track as you go, it's a fantastic idea to have a weekly meal planning session.

Monitor your development: Lastly, you'll need an effective method to monitor your development. Unless losing weight is your main objective, this doesn't necessarily have to be your weight. Tracking your blood sugar, ketone levels, waist size, and other metrics might be a good idea, depending on your motivation for going keto.

Typical keto errors and how to prevent them

Here are a few of the most typical keto errors and some troubleshooting tips.

Overindulgence in carbs

You may easily exceed your daily carbohydrate allowance while following an extremely low-carb diet like the ketogenic diet. This is particularly true if you don't have a food diary or app open to log your meals or portion amounts.

Three tactics to help you avoid consuming too many carbohydrates are as follows:

Check labels: To find out how many carbohydrates are in each packaged product you consume, be sure to read the labels on all of your food or use a meal monitoring app. Certain dishes, particularly those that include dressings, condiments, sauces, and gravies, might have surprisingly high carb counts.

Make sure you're measuring portion sizes when you take measurements of them. We are all not very good at calculating portion sizes, according to research, which might cause problems while following a ketogenic diet. Using a food scale is the most accurate method to measure portion sizes.

Maintain a food journal. Lastly, you should record every mouthful of food and liquid you consume. Even though snacks and occasional nibbles may easily be overlooked or forgotten, they can soon pile up and have a significant influence on your daily carb intake. Make sure you document everything.

Excessive Fat

Despite the high fat content of the ketogenic diet, consuming too much fat might impede weight reduction efforts. Even while your body becomes more adept at burning fat when you're in ketosis, if dietary fat is available, your body will always use it before stored body fat.

Therefore, cutting down on the fat is a smart option if you discover that you are not losing weight at the rate that you would want.

Insufficient Protein

Maintaining your muscular mass and feeling full are two benefits of protein. You may not be receiving enough protein on the keto diet if you're feeling peckish.

You should aim to consume 20–30 grams of protein, or around four ounces (about the size of your hand) of meat, with each meal and snack.

Side Effects of a Ketogenic Diet and How to Reduce Them

Following a ketogenic diet is healthy and devoid of negative effects for many individuals. Nevertheless, it's critical to recognize the "keto flu" when you first begin.

Neither the keto flu nor the flu itself are recognized medical conditions. In the keto community, this moniker was coined to describe a group of symptoms that are typical while your body is initially transitioning to keto. Among them are:

Weary

fog in the brain

Headaches

cramping in the muscles

Electrolyte abnormalities are assumed to be the cause of these symptoms. A significant amount of water weight is lost when you enter ketosis. Your body also eliminates electrolytes as a result of this water loss.

Drink lots of water (one gallon per day is recommended by many) and take supplements containing electrolytes like magnesium, potassium, and salt to help avoid keto flu.

CHAPTER TEN

Chapter 10.Risks and Measures to Take Before Beginning a Keto Diet

While many individuals find keto to be safe, there are a few things to think about before you begin, particularly if you fit into any of the following categories:

You have been diagnosed with a medical condition: keto may have an impact on your blood pressure, blood sugar, and cognitive abilities. Therefore, before beginning the program, you should speak with your healthcare practitioner if you have any disorders that are associated with these (such as type 2 diabetes, high blood pressure, or epilepsy).

You're pregnant or nursing: Adopting a ketogenic diet may be riskier and more challenging during these times. A paleo-style diet high in real foods and low in processed carbohydrates could be a preferable choice.

You're very active: If you abruptly transition to a ketogenic diet when you're very active, you may first feel fatigued and see a decline in your performance. In this situation, contacting a personal trainer or certified nutritionist with expertise in ketogenic diets and sports performance can be a very good idea.

If you use prescription drugs, keto may have an adverse effect on them. The diet, for instance, may decrease blood pressure and blood sugar levels, but this may be hazardous if you simultaneously take blood pressure or blood sugar-reducing drugs. In order for your doctor to change your medication as necessary, they must be informed of your intentions to start keto.

Never forget to consult your healthcare practitioner before beginning a ketogenic diet if you are unsure. If any of the above apply to you, it's crucial that you avoid jumping into keto immediately since it may have a significant negative impact on your health.

Is it safe to eat keto?

Many individuals may safely use keto. However, you should be mindful of the possibility of developing the "keto flu" due to changes in fluid and electrolyte balance that happen when you begin the diet. Keto flu may be avoided by consuming plenty of fluids and using electrolyte supplements.

Additionally, you should speak with a healthcare professional before beginning a ketogenic diet if you are pregnant, breastfeeding, using prescription medication, or are physically active.

On the keto diet, how much weight can I expect to lose?

The amount of weight you need to lose and the degree of your calorie deficit have a major role in this.

Even on a ketogenic diet, you must eat fewer calories daily than you burn off in order to lose weight. The ideal strategy to do this is to increase your calorie-burning activity and set modest calorie restrictions for your diet. Additionally, muscle burns more calories while at rest, so strength exercise may help you gain muscle.

How can I tell if I'm in ketosis?

You may determine if you are in ketosis in a few different ways:

Ketone urine strips: they are easy to use and reasonably priced. Your urine's ketones are measured. They are useful when you initially start the ketogenic diet, but even while you are in ketosis, your body will eventually get more adept at burning ketones, so you won't see as many in your urine.

Test for ketone bodies in the breath: This test quantifies the amount of ketones in your breath. It's more dependable for those who are new to keto, much like urine testing.

Blood ketone test: This is the most costly test but also the most dependable for all individuals. You will need ketone testing strips designed especially for use with a blood ketone meter.

What distinguishes low-carb from ketogenic diets?

"Low carb" refers to any diet, including keto, that has 130 grams or less of carbohydrates per day or less. But not all low-carb diets are keto; only those with a carbohydrate content low enough to encourage ketosis qualify as such.

Certain low-carb diets nevertheless have too many carbohydrates in them to allow you to enter ketosis.

What is the ideal duration for a ketogenic diet?

You have the last say on this. Many claim to have followed a ketogenic diet for years without success. Some decide to stick with keto until they reach their health objectives, at which point they switch to a less stringent diet.

The Clue to Why Keto Is Effective

Although the keto diet is straightforward, it might take some time to get used to it. It takes a significant shift in both your physiology and lifestyle to switch from consuming all the high-carb meals you want to filling up on fat for fuel.

Is the trek towards keto worth it in the end? Depending on the individual,.

High-quality studies on the keto diet have shown that it regularly leads to the same amount or slightly greater weight loss as many other popular diets, and for many, the answer is an unequivocal and resounding "yes." Additionally, the most recent study suggests that keto may be able to aid with a number of the prevalent illnesses that people now face, including Alzheimer's disease, type 2 diabetes, and heart disease.

These amazing outcomes are mostly due to two mechanisms:

It lowers calorie intake organically. Eat more highly-satisfying real foods and limit processed meals that stimulate appetite—this is what the keto diet promotes. Many keto dieters feel full all day long as a result, which means they don't need to consume as many calories as they did previously. This natural cutback in energy intake usually results in decreased body weight and improved levels of many biomarkers associated with heart disease and type 2 diabetes.

It leads to more ketone usage. In many respects, ketones are the most effective energy source we have, but they can't be generated until we don't have enough sugar in our bodies to maintain brain activity. Ketones have numerous beneficial consequences for our bodies when we burn them for fuel. These advantages include reduced hunger, more energy, and improved brain health (you can read more about these benefits by clicking this link).

What distinguishes the keto diet above anything else is its potent mix of ketone generation and sustained calorie reduction. Additionally, you are free to follow it for as long as you choose (we will look at this in more detail later in this post).

However, you have to go over the most difficult portion of most deaths in order to reach your objectives for body composition and health.

plans: initiating the process. Thankfully, switching to a ketogenic diet isn't tough if we weed out all the superfluous information and simplify it into three simple stages.

Made in the USA
Coppell, TX
25 October 2024

39161811R00069